C000170983

WALM

AND ITS SURROUNDINGS

BY DOUGLAS V. JONES

Walmley Ash Road at its junction with Walmley Road and Eachelhurst Road

Westwood Press Publications

44 BOLDMERE ROAD, SUTTON COLDFIELD
WEST MIDLANDS B73 5TD
TELEPHONE: 021-354 5913

Acknowledgments

The author and publisher thank Birmingham Central Library for the use of photographs from the Benjamin Stone collection and the undermentioned for their help with illustrations and information in this book:

Mr Arthur Abbott; Mr John Bassett; Mr W.A. Butler; Mr Harry Collins; Mr Ben Davis; Mr J.P. Gilmour; Mr Colin Green; the Rev. Barry Harper, B.Sc., Vicar of Walmley; Mr Paul Holden Ll.B; Mr E.S. Holder; Col. John H.C. Horsfall, D.S.O., M.C; Mrs Pauline Jenns; Mr A. Lever; Mr H.V. McConnell; Mr E.S. Russell; Mrs Margaret Sargent; Dr Ian and Mrs Joyce Shearer; Miss E. Spencer; Mr D.A.Spinks; Mrs L.V. Thompson; Mr Richard Wallis and Mr G. Whitehouse.

FRONT COVER

The post-card, reproduced on the cover, was published for Mrs E.A. Butler, who was Walmley's post-mistress from 1924 to 1938. Her son and her grandson later held the office of post-master. Her grandson, Mr W.A. Butler, still lives in the village.

ISBN 0 948025 11 5

© Copyright Westwood Press
Early Summer 1990

Printed by The Westwood Press, 44 Boldmere Road Sutton Coldfield. Produced by offset litho.

Contents

Walmley's shopping centre

These two aerial views of Walmley in the early 1930's illustrate graphically the rural surroundings of the village at that time

CHAPTER I

Walmley and Penns

WHEN THE RECORDED HISTORY of a place is obscure, we look to other means of finding out something of its past. Place-names are sometimes revealing, sometimes perplexing. The name 'Walmley' might be said to be both. 'Ley', or 'lea' denotes a field, while 'Walm' may be a corruption of 'Home'. This gives us 'home field', with Langley at the far end of Fox Hollies Road as the 'far field'. These fields or enclosures in a sparsely populated region suggest early settlements.

Langley, the site of Langley Hall, splendidly moated and crenellated though long since gone, is well documented. But the origin of the 'home' of 'home ley' remains obscure. We can only surmise that it was a small, unimportant settlement, unworthy of a mention in the Domesday Book, and such it long remained. It centred on an inter-section of roads with a few scattered houses: a mere hamlet on the outskirts of the parish of Sutton Coldfield rather than a village. It had no church, no inn and no assembly point of any sort.

Walmley's rating as an obscure hamlet was emphasised in 1879 when the Midland Railway Company built a line through it. Its station was called, not Walmley, but Penns, in recognition of the fact that it was Penns Mill which had, in past times, brought industry to an otherwise poor agricultural area. Nearby Minworth had a much higher rating, with a village status dating back to Saxon times.

The roads in and around Walmley were dreadful, and John Horsfall in his book, *The Iron Masters of Penns,* recalls that in his youth they were merely unmade-up country tracks, and he remembers the suffocating clouds of dust rising around a 1905 vintage Lanchester, driven by the chauffeur from New Hall 'at a reckless 25 mph'.

With so short a history it is, perhaps, not surprising that both antiquity and architectural merit should be lacking in the buildings along Walmley Road through the modern extended village. Even the parish church of St. John only dates from 1845. Designed by D.R. Hill in the Norman style, it is not highly

Walmley Village early in the twentieth century

rated by the connoisseurs of church architecture. Nikolaus Pevsner in the Warwickshire volume of *The Buildings of England* speaks of it disparagingly and reminds us that it is built entirely of the dark blue vitrified bricks now cherished as engineering bricks. Only the Norman shafts and arches, he adds, are of stone.

A new, more spacious church has recently been built beside and adjoining the old. At the time of going to press the old church is in the process of being converted into a church centre. At ground level there will be a lounge, with the chancel converted into a small chapel. The upper floor will be a hall for church meetings and other functions. The old hammer beam roof, Norman arches and beautiful stained-glass windows are to be retained.

The Fox Inn in the middle of the village is a modern hostelry, which was built to replace an earlier inn. The almshouses at the junction of Walmley Road and Fox Hollies Road date from several different periods. The four little dwellings nearest the junction were erected early in the 19th century. Later ones were built in 1924 and others in 1971, on which occasion Princess

The cross roads—at the junction of Penns Lane, Walmley Road, Eachelhurst Road and Walmley Ash Road

St. John's Church, Walmley

Interior of St. John's Church

8

Among the various memorials in St. John's Church are a reading desk and plaque, commemorating the life of Second-Lieutenant Noel Forge, aged 19, who was killed in action near Cambrai in 1917. According to the official citation he died whilst 'most bravely and gallantly trying to save his men.' He was the son of the then Vicar of Walmley, the Rev. J.F.Forge

Anne came to Walmley for the opening ceremony, when she unveiled a commemorative plaque. The name of the administrative building, Lingard House, recalls the name of a benefactress, Frances Lingard, a 19th century Sutton Coldfield spinster.

Walmley's first school was a charity school, financed from funds impounded by the Courts in 1792 in respect of acts of alleged mismanagement by Sutton Coldfield Corporation over a long period of time. The money was released by the Lord Chancellor's office in 1825 and used, with the Court's approval, for founding elementary schools in the town. The school was built in that part of Fox Hollies Road known as 'Beyond the Wood', and with it was erected an adjoining house for the school mistress, whose salary was £25 a year, plus a free supply of coal. This school, providing for the needs of 60 children, continued until 1851, when a bigger school was built adjacent to the church and the charity school was then converted into two cottages.

Walmley's several modern schools are all pleasantly situated and wide-ranging in their curricular activities. Walmley First School in Walmley Ash

Walmley's old parsonage was built in 1843 and demolished in the early 1970s, when the present vicarage was built

The Village, Walmley c. 1930

Road was built in 1956, when the infants from the old Village School were transferred to the new premises. The juniors remained in the old school prior to the building of Walmley Middle School some years later. Described as 'a happy educational environment', these two schools, with their large playing-fields and a nature reserve, occupy land used for an Italian prisoner-of-war camp during the Second World War.

The Deanery Church of England Aided First and Middle Schools in Fox Hollies Road, which are supported by the churches in the Sutton Coldfield Deanery, were built in 1980. They serve the needs of Walmley's ever-growing population, drawn from the nearby new housing estates.

Walmley, like any other village in close proximity to a large conurbation, has seen many changes in recent years. Extensive development of surrounding green belt land for housing has destroyed much of its rural aspect and the huge increase in traffic has called for measures to accommodate it. A long running battle ensued between the highway authorities and the residents over the need or otherwise for road widening in the village.

Walmley Road was described as a 'commuter route' into Birmingham for the inhatitants of Sutton and surrounding towns and was said to be one of the most heavily trafficked roads in the district. But the majority of Walmley residents were vigorously opposed to road widening. In 1967 the Sutton Coldfield Civic Society took up their cause when they pointed out that widening would destroy the village atmosphere and that it would be contrary to the spirit of the Civic Amenities Act. Possibly as a consequence of this opposition widening was confined to the cross-roads at Penns Lane and Walmley Ash Road and the installation there of traffic-lights.

With a present population of 27,000 and still rising, Walmley has been called Sutton Coldfield's 'boom suburb'. But, unfortunately, its existing services are inadequate. More schools and better roads are now demanded. Plans have been approved for a by-pass in 1991. This will run in a broad sweep from Walmley Road, (B.4148) at a point near New Hall lodge, to Walmley Ash Road, crossing Springfield Road and Signal Hayes Road. It will thus gain access, via the A.38 to the city centre, or to the M.42 / M6 Motorways, providing a complete by-pass for Walmley Village.

* * * * * *

Penns in 1817

Penns Lake in 1860

For history nearest to hand we have to look westwards for half a mile from the cross-roads, down Penns Lane to the crossing of the Ebrook, now called Plants Brook. Here, in the 18th century, beside the stream, began a colourful story when Joseph Webster, a wire-drawer, rented a mill at Penns where, to increase the power of the stream for milling purposes, he made a large mill-pond. The work was done over a long period of time by men armed only with spades and barrows. The end product, apart from its utility value, was a sheet of water of great beauty, graced by water-fowl and fringed by trees, still a source of pleasure to local people and visitors alike.

It was an era of burgeoning industry in the West Midlands and the contribution of Webster and his successors was considerable. They had other milling and forging sites in the district at Minworth, Perry Barr and Hints. At Penns, despite the sparse population of the region, they apparently had no difficulty in recruiting labour. Some of that labour, we know, was from outside the parish, for the Overseers of the Poor, mindful, of the need to avoid non-parishioners becoming a charge on the rates should they become paupers, made known their concern. John Horsfall in *The Ironmasters of Penns,* tells us that Joseph Webster bound himself in the sum of £40 to indemnify the church wardens at Sutton against any charges or claims in respect of five of his men.

Penns in 1936, north aspect. The site of the old mill is in the trees on the right

Discarded old crucible pots were for long to be seen in considerable numbers around farm buildings in the Fox Hollies region of Walmley

With no railway, no navigable waterway and appalling roads, transportation of raw material was a problem. The pig iron used in the making of wire came from the Forest of Dean. It was bought at Chepstow and conveyed by river and wagon to Penns. The situation was eased after the completion of the Birmingham — Fazeley Canal in 1783, which passed beside the Webster's forge at Minworth.

The manufacturing process was greatly improved when Webster used the unpatented invention of Benjamin Huntsman, (1704-1776), a Doncaster watch-maker who had had difficulty in making springs for his watches. In a crucible pot and using a handful of charcoal he produced a cast steel purer than any then in use. The invention was of great importance to Webster in the making of high grade steel wire. Discarded old crucible pots were for long to be seen in considerable numbers around farm buildings in the Fox Hollies region of Walmley.

The Webster dynasty at Penns continued until 1855, when another Joseph Webster, (the third), went into partnership with James Horsfall, who had successfully developed and produced a high-tensile piano wire, which he had patented. The success of the merger soon became apparent and the firm of Webster and Horsfall — now of Hay Mills, Birmingham — is still in business. Production at Penns Mill ceased in 1859, when the firm moved to Hay Mills.

The closure caused unemployment and hardship in the district and by 1860 the population of Walmley had dropped by 100.

But the end of milling did not terminate the Horsfall connection with Penns. For many years members of the family lived there, they having acquired the house at Penns in 1865. Henry Coldwell Horsfall died in 1941 and his widow survived until 1947. After her death the property was bought by local brewers and the site of Penns House is now occupied by the prestigious Penns Hall Hotel.

Oak Farm in Walmley Ash Road, after having been sold in 1948,
was demolished in 1979 to make way for a new housing estate

LOT 5

Valuable Freehold Agricultural Property

KNOWN AS

"Oak Farm"

Walmley Ash Road, Walmley

Very conveniently situated about ½-mile from Walmley Village, with CAPITAL
HOUSE, extensive FARM BUILDINGS and 104 ACRES 2 ROODS 20 PERCHES
or thereabouts of excellent ARABLE AND PASTURE LAND, having a frontage
of approximately 385 yards to Walmley Ash Road.

Let to Messrs. S. E. and C. H. Bates on Annual Lady Day tenancy at an apportioned
Rental of £186 12s. 0d. per annum.

TOGETHER WITH

A PAIR OF FREEHOLD COTTAGES, situate in Fox Hollies Road, separately let
and producing £38 7s. 0d. per annum gross.

JONES'S WOOD (O.S. No. 2764), 5.979 ACRES, is in hand and will also be
included with the Farm; making the Total Area

111 ACRES 1 ROOD 1 PERCH,

or thereabouts, and the TOTAL RENTALS RECEIVABLE £224 19s. 0d. per
annum.

Extract from the sale catalogue relating to the sale of Oak Farm in 1948

Scenes from Walmley's Past

The Fox Inn, Walmley, which was demolished and rebuilt in the early 'thirties

The pleasure garden of the Fox Inn

Walmley's tug-of-war team, 1922

The war memorial and almshouses, Walmley. The war memorial paid for by public subscription, was unveiled in 1920

Penns Lane in quieter times

These two cottages in Penns Lane, now demolished, were built by Joseph Webster in 1812 to accommodate workers in nearby Penns Mill

The wall-plaque reads J.W. 1812

Henry Herbert Coldwell Horsfall leaving Penns for Hay Mills, Easter 1909

Walmley's second school stood next to the church
It was built in 1851 and demolished in 1975

Walmley Junior School

The date of this early 20th century photograph is not known

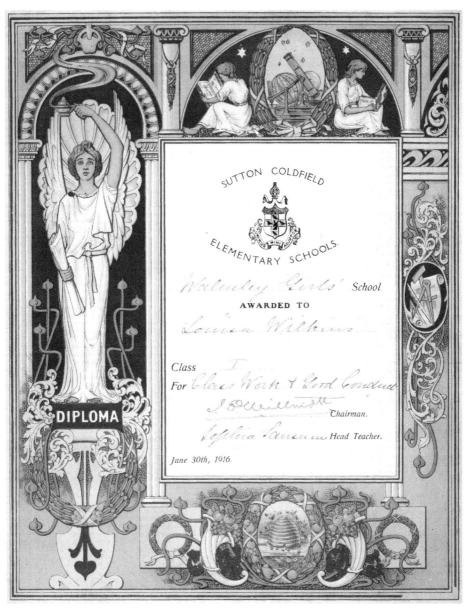

SUTTON COLDFIELD

ELEMENTARY SCHOOLS.

Walmley Girls' School

AWARDED TO

Louisa Wilkins

Class *I*

For *Class Work & Good Conduct*

J. Willmott Chairman.

Sophia Sansum Head Teacher.

June 30th, 1916.

DIPLOMA

Diploma awarded to Louisa Wilkins, a pupil at Walmley Girls' School, in 1916

Penns Station in 1949. The old Midland line through Walmley ceased to carry passengers in 1964. The station has since been demolished. Photo by E.S. Russell (Courtesy John Bassett from 'Cross City Connections')

Walmley Village in 1965

CHAPTER II

New Hall, New Hall Mill and the Ebrook

Moated and splendidly set amid its own woodland, the name of New Hall is something of a misnomer for a building claimed to be the oldest inhabited house in England. The first hall was built on the site around 1200, but was later rebuilt, which may account for it having been known as 'New Hall' for some 600 years. Additions were made to the building in both the eighteenth and nineteenth centuries.

In the course of its long existence New Hall has changed hands many times. In Edward III's time it was possessed by William de Sutton of Warwick, a kinsman of the Warwick Earls. Other names flicker across the pages of history: in the sixteenth century William Gibbons, a brother-in-law of Bishop Vesey and first Warden of Sutton Coldfield under its Royal Charter in 1528, occupied the Hall. The estate later passed to the Sacheverells and then to the Chadwicks, whose occupancy continued until the late nineteenth century.

In 1885 New Hall became a boys' boarding school. The large upper rooms were said to have made excellent dormitories and the lower ones were converted into class-rooms to cater for the educational needs of between sixty and seventy pupils. When, by 1903, the school ceased to be financially viable, the hall was sold to Walter Wilkinson of Wilkinson and Riddell, wholesale drapers. Walter Wilkinson occupied it for many years. It was he who brought the picturesque black and white timber-framed 'Wincelle' from Wigginshill in 1910 and rebuilt it on the New Hall estate, where it can be seen from Wylde Green Road, on the Walmley side of the stream, just beyond the bridge.

Walter Wilkinson's poor blind wife is still remembered, in her old age, as being in the habit of riding round the grounds of New Hall in a little donkey-cart, a wicker work vehicle with two large wheels at the back and two small ones at the front. Her sightless and solitary pleasure in her surroundings was made possible by the co-operation of the donkey, more trac-

*Moated and splendidly set amid its own woodland, New Hall
has changed hands many times*

*New Hall was a boys' boarding school from 1885 to 1903.
This photograph was taken by Benjamin Stone in 1892*

table than most of its kind, which completed the circuit of the estate without goading, having been trained successfully to do the trip unaccompanied.

In 1923 New Hall became the home of the Owen family. Alfred Owen was an engineer and industrialist who, with a man named Rubery, founded a firm which was to make the name Rubery Owen known internationally as makers of car components. Alfred Owen died in 1929. His son and heir, another Alfred — later Sir Alfred — is still remembered by many local people. He was chairman and joint managing director of Rubery Owen, which became the biggest privately owned business in Britain. Sir Alfred Owen was mayor of Sutton Coldfield in 1951-52, a freeman of the town and a lay preacher. His love of fast cars led him to the possession of three Bentleys and the sponsorship of the BRM racing car. He died in 1975.

New Hall was owned by Michael Blakemore for a short period in the early 'eighties before being bought by Thistle Hotels and converted into a country house hotel and restaurant. The necessary alterations and extensions for the conversion have been carried out tastefully and both the imposing character and the atmosphere of New Hall have been retained.

* * * * * *

New Hall, despite its name, is claimed to be the oldest inhabited house in England

*Viewed from any angle the black and white timber-framed 'Wincelle'
in Wylde Green Road, is picturesque*

*'Wincelle' in its skeletal form, photographed in 1910, when it was being removed
from Wigginshill to Wylde Green Road. 'Wincelle' is the old name for
Wigginshill, under which name it appeared in the Domesday Book*
Photograph: Benjamin Stone

Other buildings on the New Hall estate are also of historical interest. Warren House Farm, on the Walmley Road boundary of the estate, now
hemmed in by modern bricks and mortar, bears on the wing of the building
the inscribed date 1671. But that, it is believed, only refers to the date of
the added wing. The house in its original state is attributed to Bishop Vesey
and is almost certainly one of the 51 stone houses he had built all around
Sutton Coldfield in the sixteenth century.

With its oak beams, thick stone walls and spiral staircase, its stone steps
worn by the feet of ages past, Warren House Farm is now the home of Dr
Ian and Mrs Joyce Shearer. The term 'farm' still has a relevance, for they
have a small holding, alive with free range hens and ducks, and in adjoining
stabling they cater for the needs of 20 horses.

A quarter of a mile over the fields from Warren House Farm is the abandoned New Shipton Farm, with its large, ancient timber-framed barn, now
a listed Grade II building. On the Wylde Green Road frontage of the estate

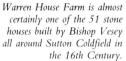

Warren House Farm is almost certainly one of the 51 stone houses built by Bishop Vesey all around Sutton Coldfield in the 16th Century.

The term 'farm' still has a relevance. The small holding at Warren House Farm is alive with free range hens and ducks and there is stabling for 20 horses.

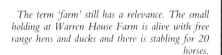

With its oak beams, thick stone walls and spiral staircase, its stone steps worn by the feet of ages past, Warren House Farm is now the home of Dr Ian and Mrs Joyce Shearer.

Photographs by James Caldwell, L.B.I.P.P.

31

The ford-keeper's cottage Wylde Green Road, in 1892,
photographed by Benjamin Stone

stands another Vesey house. Close by the stream, it was once a ford-keeper's cottage. The keeper was one of Vesey's minions, whose job it was to conduct travellers across the stream which, in earlier times, before the building of a bridge, was made treacherous by running sand and marsh.

Among the less tangible tourist attactions around New Hall is the ghost of New Shipton Farm. This, it is said, is that of a local youth who came to an untimely end over two centuries ago. The year was 1745 and the event which led to his death was the march into England from Scotland of 'Bonnie Prince Charlie', Pretender to the English throne.

An army under the Duke of Cumberland was sent in pursuit of the Pretender. At Tyburn, an advance party, having lost their way, made enquiries of a man who, having no roof to his mouth, was unable to make himself understood. He was presumed to be a spy and summarily executed on the orders of the officer in charge of the party. The poor victim's body was thrown into a ditch at Eachelhurst and his head was carried in triumph on a halbert to New Shipton, where it was flung into an oak tree.

The ford-keeper's cottage is one of Bishop Vesey's surviving original stone houses

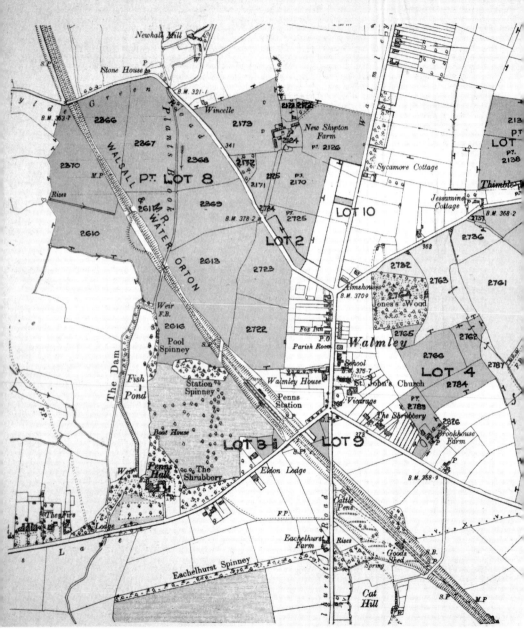

See also p

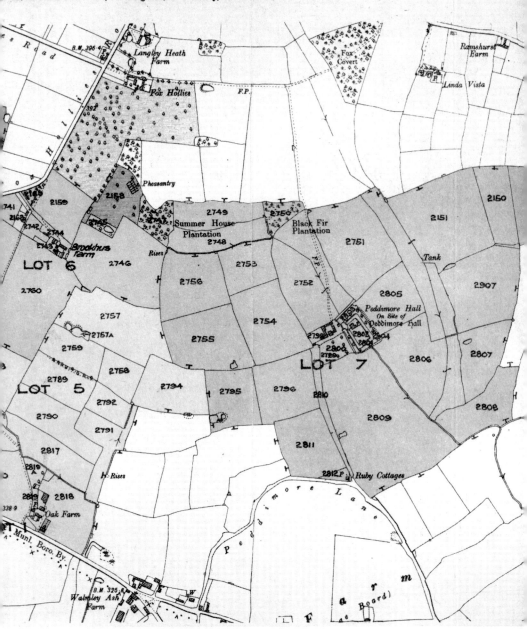

New Hall Mill was once a flour-mill

*New Hall Mill in 1907. The miller was Benjamin Styles, grandfather of
Mr Ben Davis, the present miller. It is recorded that in 1911, 32 girls and the
head mistress from Walmley School visited the mill, when the miller explained
to them the process of making flour. Mrs Styles afterwards entertained them to tea.*
Photograph: Benjamin Stone

There it remained until 1827 when the tree was felled and the skull rolled
out. And at the hour of dusk — so it has been said — the nebulous bodyless
head of this poor nameless victim of man's inhumanity to man makes its
appearance, drifting slowly across Wylde Green Road from the direction of
New Shipton, towards the scene of the crime and the spot where the body
had been so callously tossed.

★   ★   ★   ★   ★   ★

Wylde Green Road, as it looked before road-widening and showing the old brick-built bridge over the Ebrook

The Ebrook, before and after 'improvement', each photograph was taken from the bridge in Wylde Green Road, looking up stream

There were once thirteen water-mills in Sutton, but, one by one, they have disappeared and now only New Hall Mill remains as a last reminder of an earlier age. It was once a flour-mill, motivated by the Ebrook. Now, mechanically operated as a grist-mill, its old grinding stones are sunk in the pathway outside the mill and its water-wheel is rarely used. But, living in quiet seclusion with his dogs, New Hall Mill still has its resident miller, Ben Davis. He, a worthy successor of 'the jolly miller' of legend, from time to time sets the diesel engine in motion, so creating a pleasant illusion of a past industry amid halcyon surroundings.

The Ebrook rises in Sutton Park and follows a course under the town's shopping centre and through the New Hall Valley and Penns, before disgorging into the River Tame at Minworth. Until recent times its course was winding and alder-fringed, but in 1965 it fell a victim to Progress. It was no longer capable of carrying away the huge volume of drainage water from an ever-growing town and to increase its flow an 'Improvement Scheme' was put into operation. Today, straightened, concreted and, where necessary, culverted and widened, its marginal trees and much of its vegetation gone, it has a canal-like appearance which bears little resemblance to its former beauty.

Down-stream from New Hall and Penns the brook flows along the boundary of Pype Hayes Park and under Eachelhurst Road to the delightful watery setting of the Plants Brook Community Nature Park. The Nature Park's reservoirs have a history going back to the second half of the 19th century. An application to parliament by the then Birmingham Waterworks Company to obtain a water supply from Sutton Park was refused, but at a later date parliamentary approval was obtained for taking water from Plants Brook and for the sinking of wells near Plants Brook Forge at Minworth, 3½ miles downstream from Sutton.

As part of the same scheme, the reservoirs off Eachelhurst Road were made at about the same time. But following completion of the Elan Valley project in 1904, when water in abundance was piped to Birmingham from North Wales, the whole scheme was abandoned and the reservoirs served no useful purpose. The spot for long remained undisturbed and it became renowned for its peace and beauty. When in recent times, however, industrialists evinced an interest in the site, local conservationists reacted strongly to save it from the horrible fate of becoming a dumping place for toxic waste. Its future as a nature reserve now seems assured.

*   *   *   *   *   *

*Langley Hall was demolished in 1817, leaving only the moat to mark the site.
The photograph shows the moat as it appeared in 1965. It has since been drained*

CHAPTER III

Langley, Wishaw and Moxhull

THE SITE OF LANGLEY HALL lies just beyond the end of Fox Hollies Road, over a mile from Walmley Village. Its lineage is uncertain but we know that, by the thirteenth century, it was the seat of the de Beresfords of Wishaw, one of whom was Chief Justice of the Court of Common Pleas in 1289 and another a confidential retainer of the Black Prince.

Langley was a fine moated house with almost the proportions of a castle, with its own pond and fishery. It was held of the Earl of Warwick "by service of 42 shillings and two pence a year". In 1327 Edmund de Beresford, described as a 'King's Clerk', had licence to crenellate the house, so making it into a fortified building.

The Manor of Langley, with that of Wishaw, passed from the de Beresfords into the hands of a family named Hore, of whom little is recorded, then to the Pudseys, of whom we know more. Early in the reign of Henry VII the estate was inherited by Edith Hore, who, it is recorded, formed a 'special liking' for Rowland Pudsey, the younger son of Henry Pudsey of an ancient Yorkshire family. He, a student at Oxford, was described as 'a gentleman much accomplished'. By marrying Edith, Pudsey acquired for himself and his descendants the Langley estate.

When one of those descendants, Henry Pudsey, died in 1677, aged 44, his two daughters, Elizabeth and Anne, became his co-heiresses, and Jane Pudsey, the widow, remarried. Her spouse was William Wilson, (known as 'Wilson the Stonemason'), a talented architect, builder of many local houses, including Moat House, Sutton Coldfield, and sculptor of the large sandstone figure of Charles II outside Lichfield Cathedral, now being eroded away by acid rain. The monument to Henry and Jane Pudsey in Sutton Parish Church is also the work of William Wilson who, after his marriage to Jane and probably through her influence at Court, received a knighthood from Charles II.

Anne, the younger of the two Pudsey daughters, inherited Langley Hall, while Elizabeth married Lord Ffolliot, an Irish peer who, with a design by Wilson, built Four Oaks Hall, (demolished in 1898). Anne married William Jesson, the son of Sir William Jesson of Coventry. Little seems to have been recorded of Jesson's occupancy of Langley except for an isolated snippet relating to a grant to him by Sutton Corporation in 1697, allowing him to make a dam to enlarge Lindridge Pool. The rent for this was three shillings — plus six bottles of wine for the Warden of the Corporation, John Thompson.

The estate subsequently had a chequered history. It was sold by a grandson of William Jesson to Andrew Hackett and in 1815 it was bequeathed to George Bowyer Adderley who, in 1817, sold it to Sir Robert Peel. For an inexplicable reason the hall was thereafter almost immediately demolished, leaving only the sizeable remains of the moat to mark its site.

Today the spot is occupied by the modern Langley House, home of Mr and Mrs J.P. Gilmour. Close by lie traces of the moat, much overgrown, its hollow filled with moisture-loving plants with, here and there, a few pockets of water. Nearby, the rambling old building, Langley Hall Farm, was, until recently, a tangible reminder of the stately homestead it once served. Described as of 'Queen Anne style', the farmhouse has been recently refurbished and converted into what the builders term: "Twelve individually designed freehold town houses with their own gardens, sited around a landscaped communal courtyard".

★ ★ ★ ★ ★ ★

The 'Queen Anne style' Langley Hall Farm was a tangible reminder of the stately homestead it once served

Langley Hall Farm was a place of great character, much of which has been lost by its recent transformation into twelve houses

Wishaw, with its past entwined and interwoven with that of Langley and of neighbouring Moxhull, is a place of peace and quiet, out of character with the noisy and phrenetic age in which we live. With around 200 inhabitants its population has hardly fluctuated over the centuries for 900 years. In the time of Edward the Confessor, Wishaw belonged to Ordric. After the Conquest he still maintained a tenuous hold on his two hides of land there, but only as a sub-tenant of the Norman overlord, William Fitz-Corbucion.

Some land at Wishaw belonged to the Knights Templar, probably a gift from the overlord. The Templars were a religious military order, first established at Jerusalem to assist pilgrims travelling to the Holy Land. In the 13th century the Templars granted some land to Margery de Lisle, whose family held Moxhull manor for some centuries. Later, however, it changed hands many times and the manorial rights of both Wishaw and Moxhull became closely linked.

In 1843 the Manor of Wishaw was purchased by the Hon. Berkeley Octavius Noel. His successor, Berkeley Plantagenet Guildford Charles Noel, sold the estate to Thomas Ryland, a member of whose family built the present Moxhull Hall to replace an earlier building, destroyed under somewhat mysterious circumstances by fire. The house is set in well-wooded surroun-

43

Moxhull Hall, built on the site of an earlier hall, has a fine oak staircase,
taken from Kenilworth Castle and installed in the old hall in 1760

dings, its interior distinguished by splendid oak panelling. The Rylands remained at Moxhull until the 1920s, after which there were two further
owners. In 1969 the hall was converted into an hotel, the present proprietor
of which is John Boden.

Wishaw Church is dedicated to St. Chad and, according to legend, he, in
passing this way, asked the villagers where they prayed. When they replied
"In the fields" he said that was where they should have their church. The
spot is certainly an open one. The present edifice, built on the site of an earlier
place of worship, is possibly, in part, 13th century, while the tower dates
from the mid–17th century. The church underwent a restoration in 1886,
when the modern 'heavy raking' buttresses were probably added. The interior is lacking in embellishments and its strictly utilitarian, tongued-and-
grooved wooden roof panelling make it as plain as any Quaker meeting-
house.

Wishaw, like Middleton, has one unusual feature in its church — a 'leper's squint', or hagioscope. This canted orifice pierces the wall from the N.E. angle of the south aisle, and may have been used for watching the mass at the altar from the aisle in pre-reformation days. Alternatively, it could have been used for the 'confessional', through which the penitent confessed his sins to the priest, but whatever its use it does not seem likely that it was ever of any service to the unfortunate leper.

The Grove at Wishaw is a cruck-framed house of some antiquity, the origins of which have been lost to us, while the Cock Inn, said to have been a farmhouse in the 15th century, was, by the early 18th century, known to have become a public-house under the name of "The Cock and Malt Shovel".

Wishaw's Church, dedicated to St. Chad, has one unusual feature —
a 'leper's squint', or hagioscope

The present House at Peddimore only dates from 1659,
but a building has occupied the site from much earlier times.
Traces of the double moat can still be seen

CHAPTER IV

Peddimore

Peddimore Hall, once described as "a sober, serious, brooding house, still mindful of its past" was thought to be of such historic interest that, during the Second World War, the government saw fit to make a photographic record of it, lest it should be destroyed by enemy action. Happily, although a large bomb fell in nearby Walmley Ash Lane, the hall was unscathed.

Although the present house at Peddimore only dates from 1659, a building has occupied the site from much earlier times. Its double moat denoted a place of some consequence, the occupants of which would have been favourably sited for defending themselves against aggressors. The occupants were, in fact, the Peddimore Ardens, so called to distinguish them from another branch of the family in nearby Park Hall, which lay between Castle Bromwich and Water Orton. The Ardens, often referred to collectively as the Ardens of Arden, were a very old Warwickshire family, dating back a thousand years. Mary Arden, Shakespeare's mother, was a member of the family.

Thomas de Arden of Peddimore, a freeman, having found favour with Edward I., (1272-1307), took upon himself the right to use his land as he saw fit. But Peddimore was within the compass of Sutton Chase, then the domain of the Earl of Warwick, who began a law suit against Arden to restrain him. Having second thoughts, however, the earl eventually conceded the right of Arden to fish in the Ebrook, (Plants Brook), to graze his hogs in the woods of Peddimore and Curdworth, to beat down acorns for them and to gather nuts for his own use. So, through the mists of antiquity, we have this rare glimpse of Plantagenet England and one man's fought-for right vindicated.

Thomas de Arden's sturdy gesture was, perhaps, in part, attributable to the time in which it was made. Edward I., nicknamed 'Longshanks' on account of his inordinately long legs, was knowledgable in the law and a competent and popular ruler. His reign saw great and enduring reforms in the law and in the tenure of land. Not without justification he was called 'the greatest of the Plantagenets' and 'the English Justinian'.

Peddimore today is the home of Mr Richard Wallis, his wife and two daughters. The Wallis family has occupied the house since 1921. It is a building of great character as well as a beautiful and comfortable homestead. The surrounding farm is given over mainly to beef stock and cereals. There are 60 head of cattle, livery stables and over 300 turkeys, geese and ducks.

Sutton By Pass is just a stone's throw away from Peddimore Hall. When the road was made in the early 'seventies the contractors, using their heavy equipment, cleaned out a section of the double moat. At the same time 600 roach and tench were put into it and domestic ducks were introduced to help to keep the water clean. The farm's old, timber-framed barn dates from 1385 and is said never to have been altered since that date.

*   *   *   *   *   *

The canal bridge, Minworth

CHAPTER V

Minworth

At THE TIME OF THE DOMESDAY BOOK in 1086, Turchel of Warwick held four hides of land at Curdworth, with one hide at Minworth, and down the centuries Minworth has had to play second fiddle to its near neighbour, Curdworth. Minworth's proudest claim in medieval times was the possession of a water-mill, which stood on the River Tame to the south of the Water Orton road, about three-quarters of a mile from the village.

In 1783, with the building of the Birmingham to Fazeley Canal, Minworth was cut in two by this waterway, without any notable gain to itself. And almost a century later an event took place which was to leave an indelible mark upon the face of the village. In 1881 W.W. Bagot, a local landowner and a member of the family who once owned Pype Hayes Hall, sold 344 acres of land to the then Birmingham Tame and Rea Drainage Board, by which means sewage became Minworth's 'staple industry'. The project was a success from the start — at least, from the Board's point of view, if not the village's — and in 1888, Mr Bagot sold a further 358 acres of Minworth land to the Board.

If Minworth's role in the past has been a subservient one, there was at least one short period when it was on the fringe of history-making events. During the last war, when Castle Bromwich was the home of the biggest aircraft factory in Europe, Minworth had within its borders a storage depot with hangers so high that a pilot testing Spitfires habitually flew straight through them.

In 1967 Minworth suffered a great upheaval due to the need for laying a main outfall sewer to the nearby sewage works. This entailed massive excavations and tree-felling on the village green. Minworth people were very proud of this green heart to the village, which was all that remained of an eighteenth century common, and through the local press they lamented their loss. Fortunately, the village green still survives and the mellowing effect of the ensuing years has, in part, restored it to its former glory.

*The Congregational Chapel, Minworth, which stood near the canal bridge,
was built in 1855 and demolished in 1963*

Pupils at Minworth Village School, c. 1917

Many years ago Minworth was annexed by Sutton Coldfield and was administered by the town's borough council until local government reorganisation in 1974. The relationship was not always harmonious. A council plan to 'inject new life' into the village with more housing, shops and industry met with a cool reception. It became clear that many people lived in Minworth because they liked the village atmosphere and did not want to see any change.

Neither did they warm to the proposal for an 11-acre recreational development of the canal-side in the form of a 'marina'. It seems they preferred the canal to remain as it had become since its usefulness had declined — a quiet retreat from the noise and speed of traffic along the Kingsbury Road. To leave the road and descend by the steps from the hump-backed bridge to the towpath beside the canal is to leave behind the hustle and bustle of the modern age. This is the quiet world of inland waterways: a world born to serve the needs of the Industrial Revolution, but where many people now find solace in cruising along the canal at three miles an hour, or just strolling along the towpath.

Every village and hamlet should have a chronicler. Minworth is fortunate in having one but unfortunate in that the slender booklet, *In a World That*

A group of still-surviving cottages at Minworth

Steam at Minworth! Drawing a load of Jubilee trucks at Minworth Sewage Farm, this little 0-4-0 saddle-tank engine named 'Winnie' was once a familiar sight there. It was made by W.G. Bagnall Ltd. of Stafford, ran on a two-foot gauge track and belonged to the Birmingham Tame and Rea District Drainage Board

Water Orton Lane, Minworth

Has Gone by Susan Silvester, published in 1968, is now out of print. In it she captures some vivid and evocative glimpses of what life was like in the serene surroundings of Minworth in Victorian times and during the early years of this century.

She remembers the fair on the village green, with its roundabouts, coconut shies and gingerbread stall. She recalls, too, walking to Curdworth Board School with her sisters and, later, to Walmley School when, if there was snow, her mother would put old stockings over their boots. There were no school dinners then, so they had to take their own food and if they wanted a drink it had to be water.

On May Day all the local horses were decorated with coloured ribbons and braid woven into their manes and tails, with rosettes on their harness and sometimes plumes on their heads. She describes the Village Green, the playground for generations of village children. In those days, she says, it was in its natural state with a stream along one side, a pond opposite the chapel, and patches of marshy ground, where rushes grew. In the early 1900s the newly formed parish council had lime trees planted round it. About the same time a number of oil lamps were also placed around the green. A family living in the village was given the job of lighting them every night and putting them out the next morning. They were also responsible for storing them in their shed during the summer.

Striking a sombre note she tells us about funerals. All burials from the village took place at Curdworth and the coffins were usually carried by bearers. Mr Wilkins, the wheelwright, was also the undertaker and he always made the coffins. At a point about midway between Wiggins Hill Bridge and Curdworth School he would tell the bearers to rest the coffin. This was the place, according to legend, where the church was to have been built, but the Devil moved the stones every night. The spot was, and still is, known as Minworth Greaves, and the 'greaves' is, supposedly, a corruption of 'graves'.

She reminds us of the bitter winter of 1895/6, with its long spell of terrible weather, when rows of horses were waiting outside the blacksmith's shop to have frost nails put in their shoes. At the turn of the century no-one in the village had a motor-car and very few people owned traps or floats. There was no public transport before the early 1920s, when two 'buses a day began to run between Birmingham and Kingsbury on Thursdays and Saturdays.

Susan Silvester's family owned a pony and trap, which was a much envied possession. She learned to drive the pony so that she could go shopping in Erdington, where there was stabling in Station Road. Her only dread was

Minworth has had three post offices. In Victorian times the post office stood in Water Orton Lane, almost opposite the Village School. Next door to the post office was the workshop of Mr Wilkins, the wheelwright and undertaker.

*The second post office **and village shop** was in Kingsbury Road, backing on to the canal. It was demolished in the early 'seventies, when the road was realigned.*

The present post office in Water Orton Lane, facing the
Village Green

of meeting a steam-roller, which would make the pony rear and plunge in all directions. When she travelled with her husband at night the trap had two carriage lamps fixed at the front, each holding a candle in a spring-loaded cylinder. The illumination was minimal but, as she commented, they could always trust the pony to keep on the road and find her way home.

★   ★   ★   ★   ★   ★

Two views of Wigginshill's half-timbered cottage and barn, which, like its farmhouse, all date from the 17th century

CHAPTER VI

Wigginshill

WIGGINSHILL MUST VIE WITH WISHAW as the smallest and quietest hamlet
in the neighbourhood of Sutton Coldfield. Its peaceful air of rusticity belies
its closeness to Birmingham's urban sprawl. A seal is set on its antiquity by
a mention in Magna Carta.

The main buildings of Wigginshill date from the 17th century — a half-
timbered cottage with a large barn to match and a farmhouse with an in-
teresting curved gable, known as a 'Dutch gable'. It has no church, but in
1724 the Society of Friends — better known as the Quakers — bought a
plot of land and built a meeting-house and an adjoining cottage here. The
passing of the Toleration Act in 1689 had given some freedom to noncon-
formists to observe their own religious customs, and Quakers came from
all around to meetings at Wigginshill. But by the early 19th century, despite
their earlier zeal and dedication, the congregation had so dwindled that the
meeting-house was closed down and the building fell into dilapidation.

The 'hill' in Wigginshill is little more than an undulation which merely
tends to emphasise the flatness of the North Warwickshire plain, so that the
merest hummock in these parts earns the status of a hill. Across golden corn-
fields from this vantage point can be seen two humpbacked bridges over the
Birmingham — Fazeley canal and from time to time a brightly coloured barge
glides somnambulistically across a sleepy summer landscape. Far away the
tall, slender spire of Coleshill church rises as a reminder of 14th century
building skill and the faith which harnessed it.

Wigginshill has, no doubt, always been quiet, but today — served only
by a secondary road and not over-run by motor traffic — its peace is more
pronounced. Looking across the fields from beside the 300-year-old Wigginshill Farm on a summer evening, with the sweet smell of new-mown hay
filling the air, even the distant view of the tall buildings of the Castle Vale
estate against a darkening sky has an unexpected beauty.

Wigginshill Farm

The White Horse, Kingsbury Road, Curdworth

CHAPTER VII

Curdworth

LIKE SO MANY VILLAGES up and down the country, Curdworth has made the transition from ancient to modern by forming a merger of the two and, in their case, with some measure of success. Old buildings, hallowed by the weathering of centuries, mingle with the innumerable 'des.res.' of affluent or aspiring-affluent commuters and the village atmosphere is enhanced by trees and greenery of every kind to soften the outline of bricks and mortar.

One factor in retaining Curdworth's village atmosphere is its geographical position. It lies in a quiet backwater with surprisingly little through traffic, and the traveller who, attracted by a distant view of the 800-year-old church, leaves the busy Birmingham — Kingsbury road, will quickly sense the change of tempo as he enters the village. On one side of the main street stands the ancient timber-framed tithe barn and, opposite, Red Lion Cottages which, some years ago, stood empty and delapidated, have been so splendidly restored that they won a Civic Award in 1984.

Architecturally, Curdworth is dominated by the mellow sandstone edifice of its parish church. Extensively restored in late Victorian times, the interior has several features of interest for the visitor. On the north wall of the nave an unknown artist, centuries ago, painted the deep splays of the window and embellished them with various figures, including the Madonna and Child. Not surprisingly, the colour has faded, for this is believed to be one of the oldest examples of wall painting in England. Some of the colour, however, is probably of more recent origin.

On the other side of the nave is a large piece of masonry, brought here through the efforts of Lancelot Mitchell, a former Rector of Curdworth, from Water Orton's 16th century bridge when repairs were being carried out there early in this century. It bears the figure of an angel, the head of which has disappeared. This, an unusual feature to have been found in the structure of a river bridge, is perhaps attributable to the fact that the bridge was built at the behest of Sutton-born Bishop Vesey.

Curdworth Church.
Pen and ink drawing by H.V. McConnell.

The first skirmish of the English Civil War took place on the hillock
beside Curdworth Church in 1642

Curdworth has no "Bard of Avon" to draw the crowds. But it does have its association with Dr Samuel Johnson, a figure second only to Shakespeare in England's literary story. A memorial in the floor of the nave of Curdworth Church records that Cornelius and Anne Ford, who lie buried in the churchyard, and their youngest daughter, Sarah, the "dear honoured Mother" of Dr Johnson, once lived in Dunton Hall within the parish of Curdworth. The term of endearment is taken from a letter written by Johnson to his dying mother in 1759. Her death deeply affected him and his grief was mingled with guilt for not having visited her for several years, due to working in London. Dunton Hall stands beyond the Coleshill — Lichfield road, a mile from the village, a plain, brick-built house of the late 17th century.

On a plot of land beside the church is the site of the first encounter between Royalists and Roundheads at the beginning of the English Civil War in August, 1642. This was no Edge Hill or Worcester. Only a handful of men were involved in what was no more than a mere skirmish, and bloodshed was minimal. But the event is well documented, for William Dugdale, later to be the author of *The Antiquities of Warwickshire,* was there, acting as a guide to two Royalist troops of horse and one of dragoons, moving across country from Kenilworth to Nottingham, which was intercepted by a force of Parliamentarians from Coventry. According to Dugdale the Roundheads were "put to the rout" and some were taken prisoners.

At the other end of the village, along Farthing Lane, lies another pocket of pure history. Here, amid old barns and outhouses, is the site of Curdworth Hall, a moated house which disappeared long ago. Where not clogged with rubbish and overgrown with elders and nettles, traces of the moat can still be discerned, a reminder that here at Curdworth, almost a thousand years ago, was an embattled frontier between Saxon and Dane.

It is not uncommon for traces of moats to remain, long after the houses they once protected have succumbed to the passage of time, Curdworth Hall, which lay just within Saxon territory, may have been the home of Creoda — a Saxon — from whom the name of Curdworth sprang. At the time of Domesday Book in 1086, it had become Credeworde — the farm of Creoda — and by the 14th century it appeared as Cruddeworth.

Curdworth Hall was once part of a long line of fortifications, reaching from Essex to Cheshire, built in an attempt to stem the Danish incursions into the area. But the Saxons were no match for the Danish forces under Knut — more generally known as Canute — and in the year 1016, the region was over-run and plundered by the Danes.

St. Nicholas Church, Curdworth is over eight centuries old. The rounded Norman chancel arch (in picture) shows the characteristic dog-tooth mouldings of the period

This deeply-splayed window in Curdworth Church is one of several showing traces of ancient wall paintings and inscriptions

The Rev. Lancelot Mitchell, rector of Curdworth from 1905 to 1937, has been described as a 'learned antiquarian.' He is remembered for his research into local history

The fate of the defenders of Curdworth Hall is unknown, and all traces of the building have been lost, apart from a number of large pieces of dressed sandstone of local origin, built into the foundations of the farm's outhouses. And across a field, untouched by the plough in living memory, is the clear outline of a grassed-over track, leading from the site of this ancient homestead in a direct line towards Coleshill.

Like Minworth, Curdworth, too, has a chronicler. Edith Breeden is the author of two autobiographical books, *Call Back the Lovely April* and *The Rustle of Fallen Leaves*. They recall vividly the events of a long life from late Victorian times to the early 'seventies of the present century. Edith Breeden from Lewes in Sussex, a school-teacher, came to the West Midlands as a young woman, where she spent the rest of her life.

After her marriage to John Breeden, whose family farmed at Dunton, she taught for a spell at Minworth and, joining the farming community, she lived at various times at Lea Marston, Dunton Hall and the farm in Farthing Lane, Curdworth. She has left us a portrayal of life in and around Curd-

The timber-framed Red Lion Cottages, Curdworth were empty and delapidated when this photograph was taken in 1971. But in 1984 they won a civic award from the North Warwickshire Borough Council for the tasteful way in which they had been restored.

worth over a long period of time, including events during both wars, and depicts the village as it was during the inter-war years.

'The Beehive' in the middle of the village, she tells us, was much favoured by the rustics. Beside the inn was a ramshackle shed which served as the smithy, where the children coming from school, lured by the sound of the hammer on the anvil, would stand watching the leather-aproned smith as he shod the patient horses. She describes in some detail the village shop on the opposite side of the road, which carried a stock of infinite variety, as it was the only source of supply for many miles around.

The rector, the Rev. Mitchell, she tells us, was a learned antiquarian. He was: "A tall, handsome man, the name of Lancelot had been bestowed upon him in baptism, but no Guinevere had troubled the even tenor of his days. He was an avowed celibate. Knowledge of this, on his induction many years before, must surely have dashed the latent matrimonial hopes of the many maiden ladies then in his congregation".

★　★　★　★　★　★

The zig-zag bridge spanning the River Tame is
Water Orton's most celebrated ancient monument

CHAPTER VIII

Water Orton

Manor house lane, Water Orton, despite its post-war homes, looks sufficiently promising from an antiquarian point of view to still have a manor house tucked away at the end of it. Disappointingly, it fails in this promise, for the manor house was demolished just before the last war. It does, however, have *Wakefield House,* situated on the corner of Old Church Road, a fine old sixteenth-century black and white building with period chimneys to match.

Strolling along Old Church road towards the distant cluster of cooling-towers at Hams Hall, the visitor comes upon another, even older, architectural gem. This is a half-timbered house called *The Chestnuts,* believed to be in the region of a century earlier than *Wakefield House,* its style and dignity matched by a huge horse-chestnut in its grounds with a quite remarkable span, even for a county with leafy traditions, like Warwickshire.

Old Church Road is an apt name, the 'old church' having been the chapel-of-ease which once stood on a now well wooded spot, marked by old tombstones and an ancient preaching cross, consisting of a large stone base, with much worn steps and topped by a stone column five feet high. A chapel-of-ease is defined as an extra church in a large parish. Water Orton, as Sir William Dugdale, Warwickshire's county historian, recalls, was:

" . . . one of the divers petty hamlets lying on the south of the
Tame belonging to Aston-juxta-Birmingham . . . and coming under
survey with all the hamlets of Aston Parish at the Court Leet
Assembly".

Water Orton's chapel-of-ease was, according to the records, a very modest edifice in comparison with the magnificent mother church of Aston. But it continued to serve the small community until the building of the Parish Church of Saints Peter and Paul, consecrated in 1879, Water Orton having become a separate ecclesiastical parish from Aston in 1871.

The name of Water Orton denotes "a settlement upon the water". The water, of course, is the River Tame, spanned by Water Orton's most celebrated

The preaching cross, Water Orton, showing Wakefield House on the right of the picture

Coleshill Road and Watton Lane junction, Water Orton in the 'twenties

ancient monument, the zig-zag bridge, built by Bishop Vesey in the 16th century, reputedly with stones taken from Sutton Coldfield's old manor house.

Viewed from the bridge, the river has improved somewhat in appearance during recent years, and its eddying waters, once stained to a strange hue by the unspeakable filth poured into it, now runs clearer, a tribute, perhaps, to society's increasing awareness of environmental threats.

Water Orton, only eight miles north of Birmingham, has, like neighbouring parishes, grown greatly in the post-war era and has been described in official terminology as "a modern, happy and vigorous community". It has good road and rail communications, its own shops and library and ample facilities for those vigorous community members to indulge in football, cricket, tennis and bowling.

The Digby Hotel, Water Orton
Photographs by courtesy of Mr Colin Green

Many communities have their local 'worthies' — men and women whose characters and personalities live on in memory after their deaths. In Water Orton one such is Gilbert Rhodes, who died in 1982. He had a little shop and off-licence in Old Church Road and his minor eccentricities, which were usually geared to the interests of the village, earned for him the pseudonym of "Mr Water Orton".

Every time a baby was born in the village, he would raise a flag in the garden of his home with a stork on it; when the council failed in their care of the village green, he planted daffodils there, and at Christmas he ensured that the Sunday School children all had presents.

When, three years before his death, masked raiders burst into his shop and gunned him down, the village was outraged. Scores of get-well cards were delivered to his bedside and he made a remarkably speedy recovery, despite the gravity of his injuries.

Water Orton's appearance and character have been transformed by drainage and development. The osier beds and water meadows which once lay around it, together with much of the wild life associated with them, have gone. Flooding has been reduced to a minimum and the watery traditions of the hamlet known as "a settlement upon the water" survive now only in its name.

Gilbert Rhodes, who died in 1982, was once known as 'Mr Water Orton'

*   *   *   *   *   *